DO MATH WITH SPORTS STATS!

# SOCCER

## Stats, Facts, and Figures

BY KATE MIKOLEY

Gareth Stevens Publishing

**Please visit our website, www.garethstevens.com. For a free color catalog of all our high-quality books, call toll free 1-800-542-2595 or fax 1-877-542-2596.**

Cataloging-in-Publication Data

Names: Mikoley, Kate.
Title: Soccer: stats, facts, and figures / Kate Mikoley.
Description: New York : Gareth Stevens Publishing, 2018. | Series: Do math with sports stats! | Includes index.
Identifiers: LCCN ISBN 9781538211458 (pbk.) | ISBN 9781538211472 (library bound) | ISBN 9781538211465 (6 pack)
Subjects: LCSH: Soccer–Juvenile literature.
Classification: LCC GV943.25 M47 2018 | DDC 796.334–dc23

First Edition

Published in 2018 by
**Gareth Stevens Publishing**
111 East 14th Street, Suite 349
New York, NY 10003



Designer: Samantha DeMartin
Editor: Kate Mikoley

Photo credits: cover, p. 1 (main) leolintang/Shutterstock.com; cover, pp. 1–29 (clipboard) Mega Pixel/Shutterstock.com; covers, pp. 1–32 (bleacher texture) Al Sermeno Photography/Shutterstock.com; covers, pp. 1–29 (pencil) irin-k/Shutterstock.com; covers, pp. 1–29 (formula overlay) lolya1988/Shutterstock.com; covers, pp. 1–29 (index card) photastic/Shutterstock.com; pp. 3–32 (graph paper) BLACKDAY/Shutterstock.com; pp. 4–29 (paperclips) AVS-Images/Shutterstock.com; pp. 4–29 (post-its) Pixel Embargo/Shutterstock.com; pp. 4–29 (tape) Flas100/Shutterstock.com; p. 4 Natursports/Shutterstock.com; p. 5 Francis Bompard/Getty Images Sport/Getty Images; p. 7 (top) Icon Sportswire/Icon Sportswire/Getty Images; p. 7 (bottom) Scott Halleran/Getty Images Sport/Getty Images; p. 9 Jamie Squire/Getty Images Sport/Getty Images; p. 10 Kittichai/Shutterstock.com; p. 11 Fotokostic/Shutterstock.com; p. 12 Lars Baron/Bongarts/Getty Images; p. 13 nexus 7/Shutterstock.com; p. 15 Shaun Clark/Getty Images Sport/Getty Images; pp. 16, 17 Icon Sports Wire/Icon Sportswire/Getty Images; p. 18 lev radin/Shutterstock.com; p. 19 (main) Alex Menendez/Getty Images Sport/Getty Images; p. 19 (background) Kittisak Sirichunsuwan/Shutterstock.com; p. 21 Sam Barnes/Sportsfile/Getty Images; p. 22 Morne de Klerk/Getty Images Sport/Getty Images; p. 23 Norm Hall/Getty Images Sport/Getty Images; p. 25 Gareth Copley/Getty Images Sport/Getty Images; p. 26 Donald Miralle/Getty Images Sport/Getty Images; p. 27 Manchester Daily Express/SSPL/Getty Images; p. 29 Monkey Business Images/Shutterstock.com.



Printed in the United States of America

CPSIA compliance information: Batch #CW18GS: For further information contact Gareth Stevens, New York, New York at 1-800-542-2595.

# CONTENTS



Words in the glossary appear in **bold** type the first time they are used in the text.

# GET IN THE GAME

## FAST FACTS

**Statistics**, or stats, are useful to help us understand soccer. Stats are used to keep track of how well specific players and teams are doing. By looking at stats, people can quickly see what skills certain players are good at and which players may be the best overall.

The ball flies up in the air. One player jumps and hits it with her head! Another player races after it and starts kicking the ball down the field, weaving past members of the other team. She kicks the ball to another teammate, who shoots the ball straight toward the net. The other team's goalie tries to make the save, but misses. The team scores!

SOCCER PLAYERS USUALLY USE THEIR FEET, BUT THEY CAN MOVE THE BALL USING ANY PART OF THEIR BODY OTHER THAN THEIR HANDS AND ARMS. WHEN A PLAYER USES THEIR HEAD, IT'S CALLED HEADING THE BALL.

Playing soccer takes skill, energy, and strength. Many think of soccer as a low-scoring sport, but numbers still play a huge part in this action-packed game. Math is useful to help us understand the ins and outs of the sport.

# SOCCER'S EARLY YEARS

Games similar to soccer were likely first played more than 2,000 years ago. However, it would take many years for the sport to become what it is today. By the late 1800s and early 1900s, modern soccer had become popular in Great Britain and other parts of Europe. FIFA, the Fédération Internationale de Football Association (**International** Federation of Association Football), was founded in 1904 as a way to organize the sport across countries.

## PRO SOCCER IN THE UNITED STATES

In the United States, soccer is still growing as a **professional** sport. Over the years, a number of leagues have existed, but some failed. In 1996, Major League Soccer (MLS) was formed and became the most successful soccer league in the country. The National Women's Soccer League (NWSL) is the top women's professional league in the United States.

Soccer was first officially played in the Olympics in 1908 in London, England. The game continued to grow in popularity and is often considered the most popular sport in the world today.

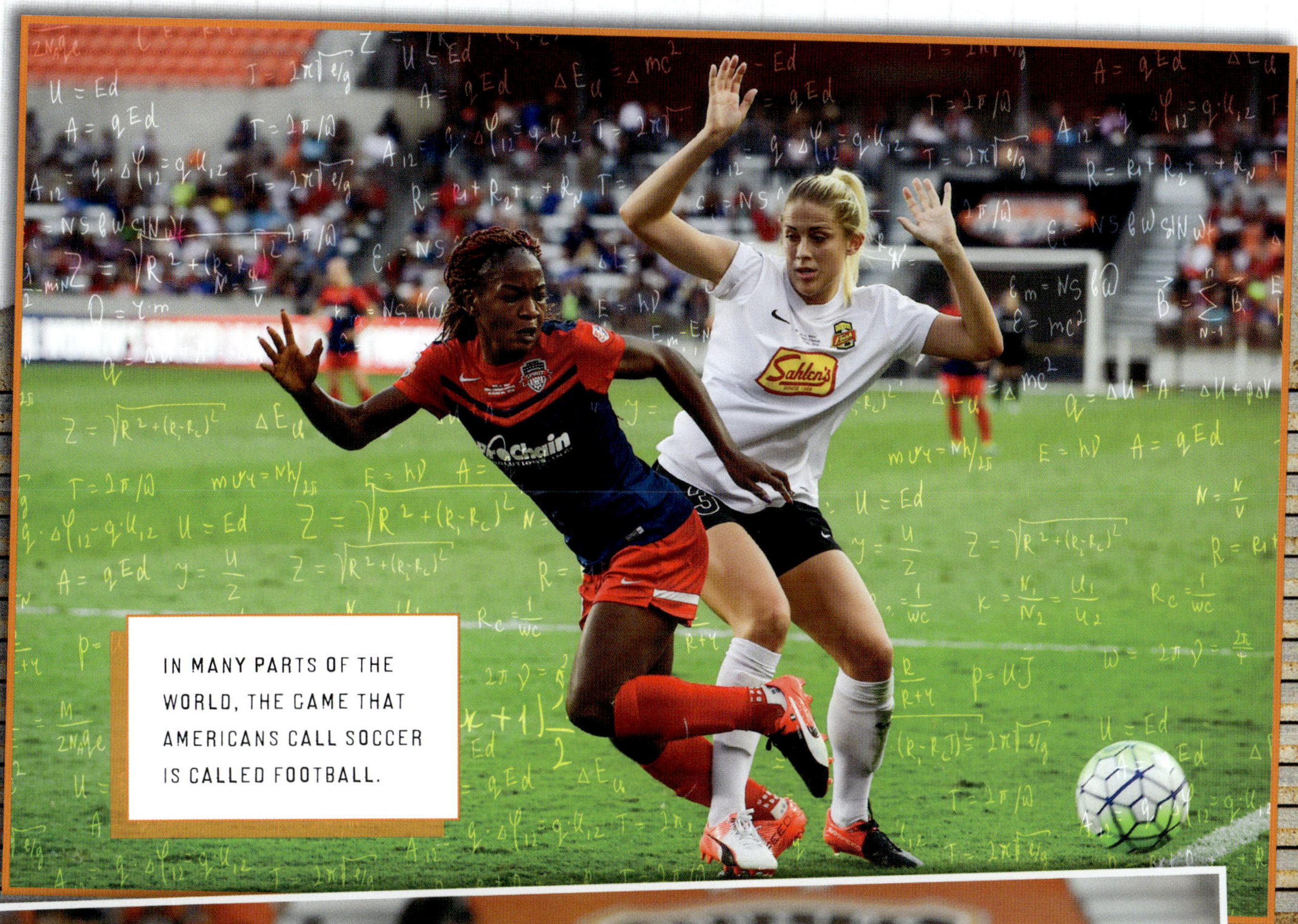

IN MANY PARTS OF THE WORLD, THE GAME THAT AMERICANS CALL SOCCER IS CALLED FOOTBALL.

# AROUND THE WORLD

Soccer may be gaining popularity in the United States, but it's still even more popular in other parts of the world. As far as numbers of players and fans, it's the number one sport on the planet, especially in countries across Europe, South America, and Africa. Teams based in England, Spain, and many other parts of the globe have fans all over the world.

## WORLD CUP NUMBERS

The World Cup has been held every 4 years since 1930, except for 1942 and 1946. Today, hundreds of teams compete to be one of just 32 teams that take part in the month-long competition. In the 2014 World Cup, held in Brazil, a total of 171 goals were scored!

The FIFA World Cup, often just called the World Cup, is a soccer **competition** between teams from all over the world. Billions of people watch the World Cup when it happens every 4 years.

BRAZIL IS THE ONLY TEAM TO HAVE PLAYED IN EVERY WORLD CUP SINCE THE EVENT'S START.

# MEASURING UP

In some sports, the areas of play need to meet exact measurements. In soccer, the fields can vary in size. In many professional and international games, the field is a rectangle between 110 yards (100 m) and 120 yards (110 m) long and between 70 yards (64 m) and 80 yards (75 m) wide.

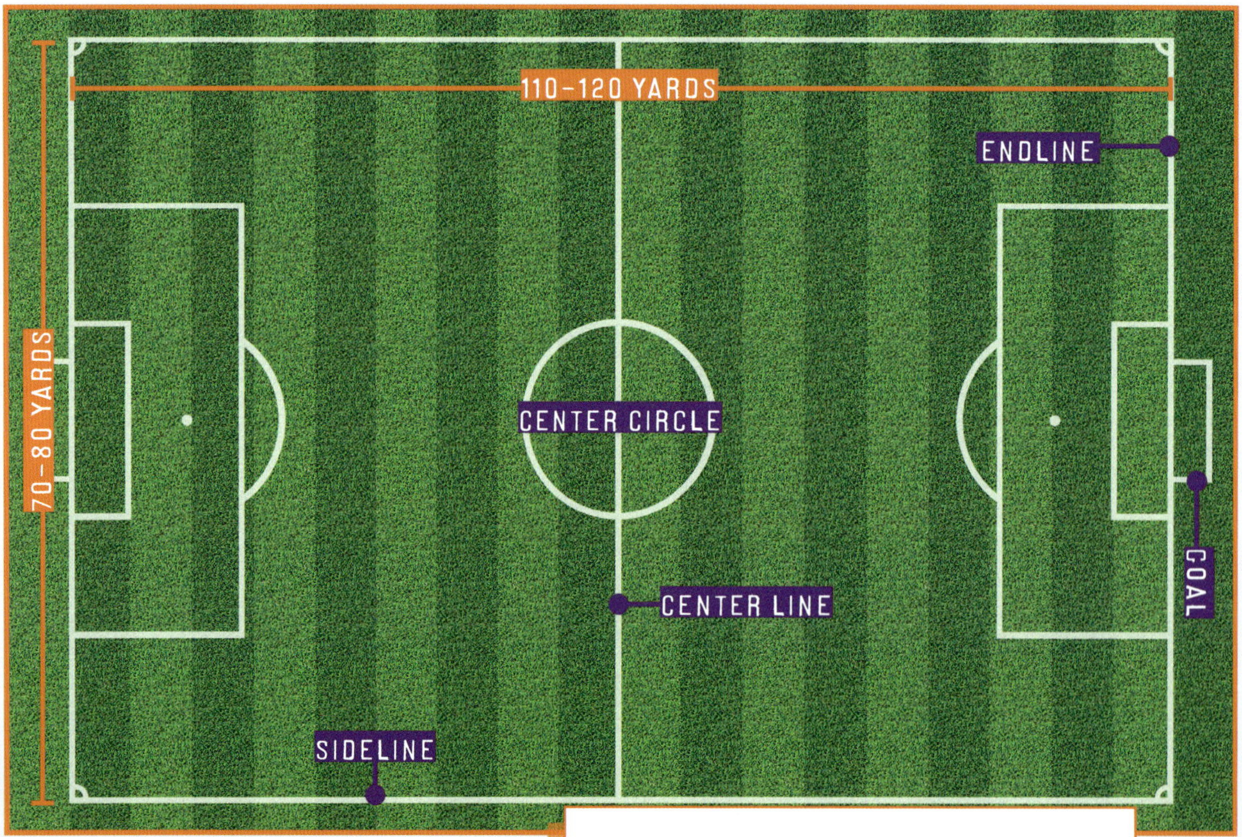


SOCCER FIELDS ARE SYMMETRICAL, OR HAVE TWO HALVES THAT ARE THE SAME. THE CENTER LINE IS THE FIELD'S LINE OF SYMMETRY.

The field is divided in half by the center line. In the middle of the center line is the center circle. At each end of the field is a goal. These are where each team tries to shoot the ball. The goalie spends most of the game guarding the net here.

## THE NUMBERS GAME

WHILE PROFESSIONAL GAMES OFTEN MUST BE PLAYED ON FIELDS IN THIS SIZE RANGE, KIDS' SOCCER GAMES ARE OFTEN PLAYED ON MUCH SMALLER FIELDS. IF A FIELD IS 55 YARDS LONG BY 40 YARDS WIDE, WHAT'S THE AREA OF THAT FIELD? REMEMBER, THE AREA OF A RECTANGLE IS **CALCULATED** BY MULTIPLYING THE LENGTH BY THE WIDTH. ANSWER ON PAGE 29.

# GET IN GOAL

The goals are important spots on the field. Each team defends, or protects, its own goal. They try to score by kicking the ball into the other team's goal. These are made up of two posts that go straight up from the ground. A bar connects the posts across the top. A net is usually attached behind the goal to catch the ball.

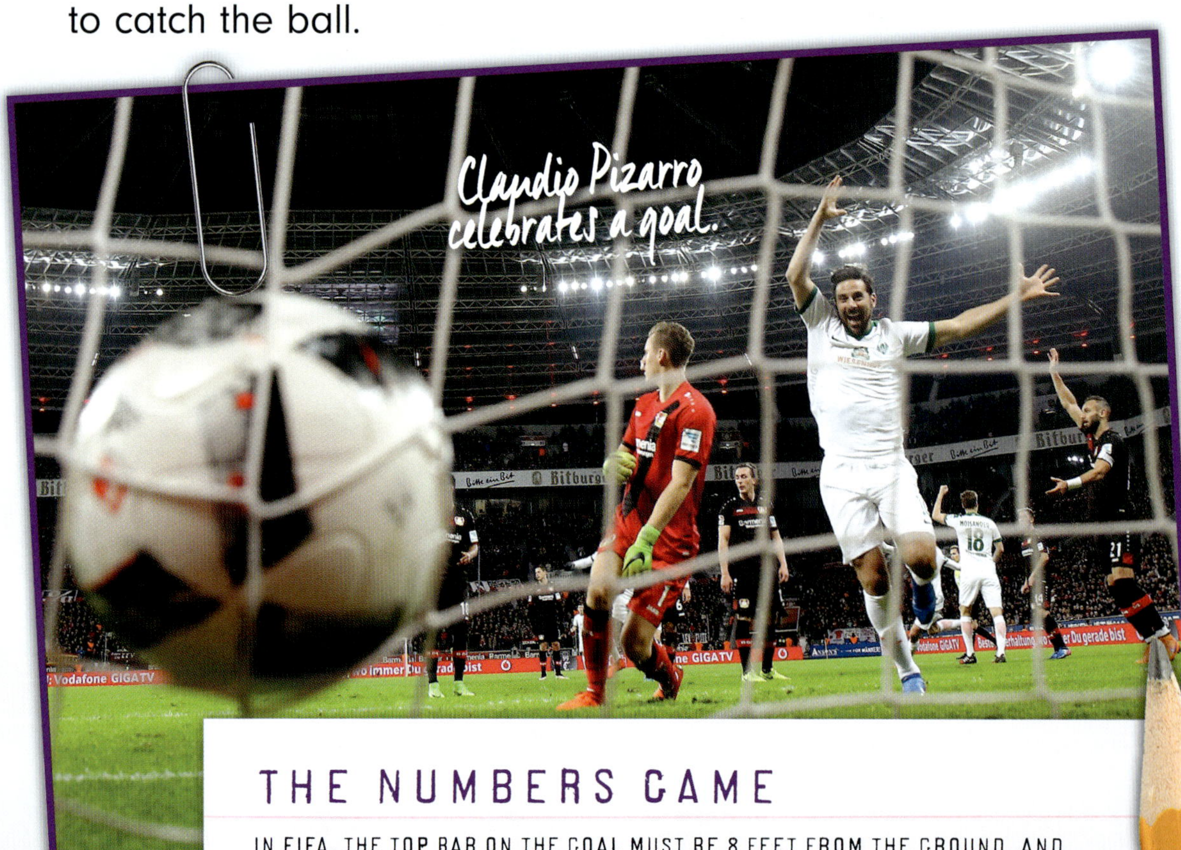

Claudio Pizarro celebrates a goal.

### THE NUMBERS GAME

IN FIFA, THE TOP BAR ON THE GOAL MUST BE 8 FEET FROM THE GROUND, AND THE TWO UPRIGHT POSTS HAVE TO BE 8 YARDS FROM EACH OTHER. IF THE POSTS ARE 8 YARDS APART, HOW MANY FEET APART ARE THEY? REMEMBER, THERE ARE 3 FEET IN 1 YARD. ANSWER ON PAGE 29.

The goals you play with might be a different size than the ones high school, college, or professional players use. A bigger goal means more space to kick the ball. This also means players trying to block the ball may have to move quicker and farther!

THE GAME TAKES PLACE ALL OVER THE FIELD, BUT THE GOALS ARE WHERE THE SCORING TAKES PLACE!

# IN POSITION

Each team is allowed to have 11 players on the field at once. One of these players is the goalie. The other 10 players consist of forwards, midfielders, and defenders. Forwards are the players who most often score goals. Defenders are players who try to keep the other team from scoring. They try to keep the ball from getting close to their goalie.

As the name suggests, midfielders most often play in the middle of the field. They're the link between the forwards and defenders. Midfielders need to have good offense and defense skills.

## THE NUMBERS GAME

IN SOME KIDS' LEAGUES, FEWER PLAYERS ARE ON THE FIELD. LET'S SAY THERE ARE A TOTAL OF 16 PLAYERS ON THE FIELD, INCLUDING ONE GOALIE FOR EACH TEAM. BETWEEN BOTH TEAMS, THERE ARE ALSO 14 PLAYERS ON THE BENCH. IF EACH TEAM HAS THE SAME TOTAL NUMBER OF PLAYERS, HOW MANY PLAYERS ARE ON EACH TEAM? ANSWER ON PAGE 29.

$$(16 + 14) \div 2$$

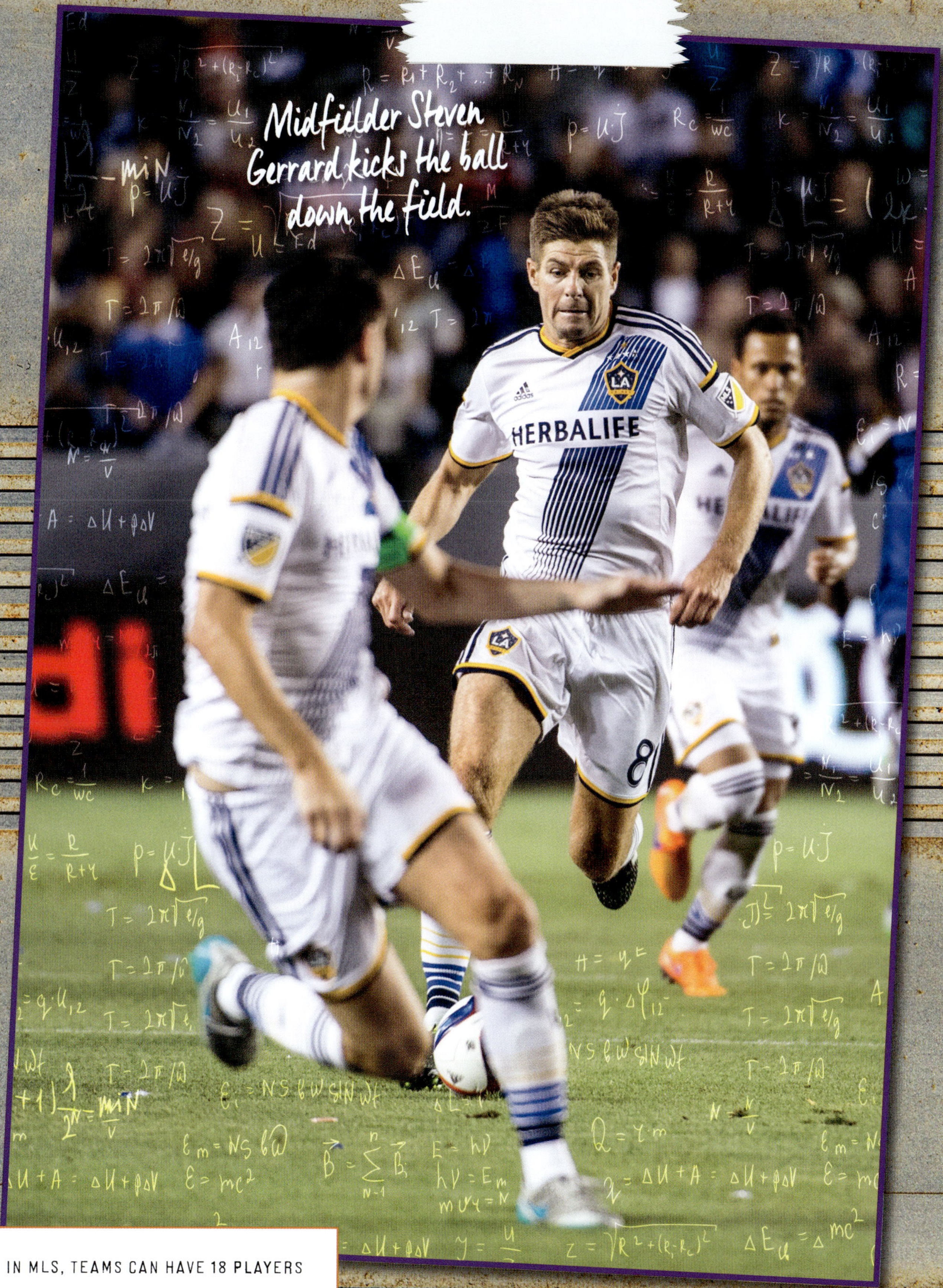

Midfielder Steven Gerrard kicks the ball down the field.

IN MLS, TEAMS CAN HAVE 18 PLAYERS ON THEIR GAME-DAY **ROSTER**.

# TAKE A SHOT

There are lots of details that go into winning a soccer game, but in the end it really comes down to one thing—goals. The team that scores the most goals wins the game, so some would say goals scored is the most important stat of all. A goal is scored when a player gets the ball past the other team's goalie and into the net.

A shot is an attempt a player makes to get the ball in the goal. A shot happens when a player kicks the ball toward the net, whether or not the shot is a goal.

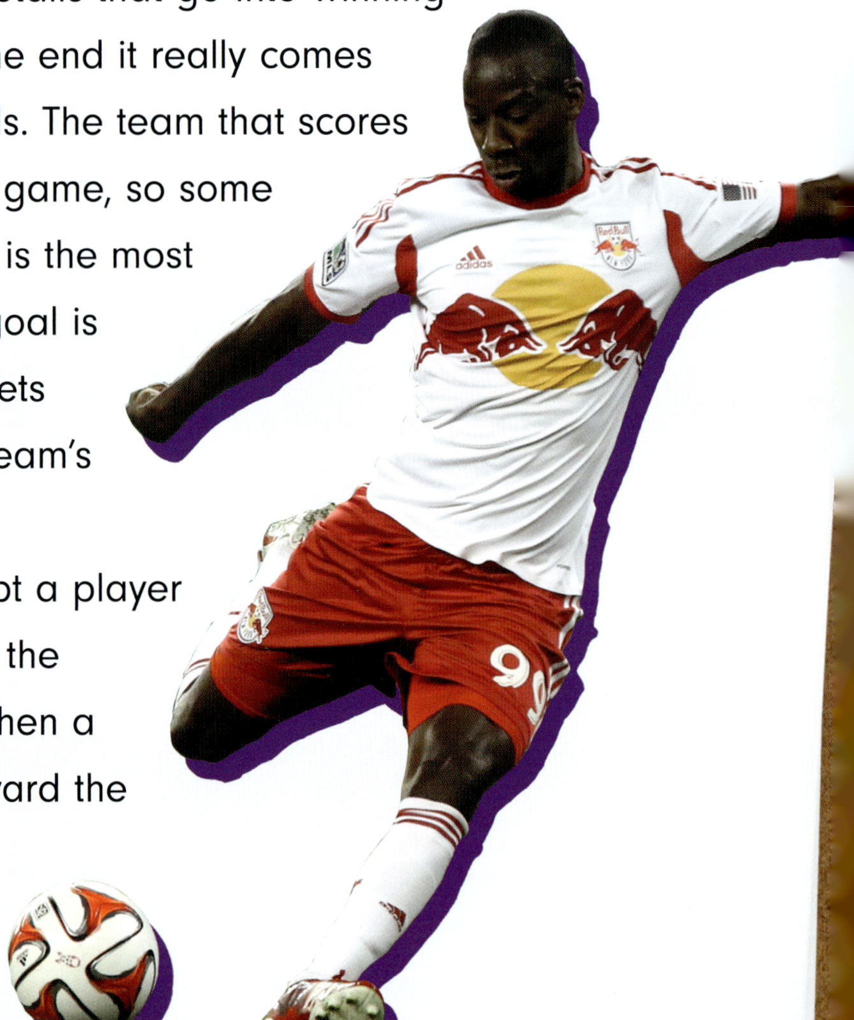

IN 2014, DURING HIS FIRST FULL SEASON WITH THE NEW YORK RED BULLS, BRADLEY WRIGHT-PHILLIPS TIED THE MLS SINGLE-SEASON GOAL SCORING RECORD BY SCORING 27 GOALS!

## THE NUMBERS GAME

THROUGHOUT A SEASON, FORWARDS MAY SCORE DOZENS OF GOALS, BUT THEY MIGHT TAKE MORE THAN 100 SHOTS! LET'S SAY A PLAYER HAS MADE 112 SHOTS. IF 1/4 OF THOSE SHOTS WERE GOALS, HOW MANY GOALS HAS THE PLAYER SCORED? ANSWER ON PAGE 29.

$$112 \times \frac{1}{4}$$

Carli Lloyd takes a shot.

A shot on goal is a shot that either does or would enter the goal if not blocked. These are shots that are on target to go into the goal. Shots on goal may be shots that go into the net and score, but not always. They're also often blocked by the goalie.

Shots on goal may not always score goals, but they can still tell us about a player's ability. Of course, it's important to get the shots in the net, but more shots on goal mean a player is making more opportunities to score.

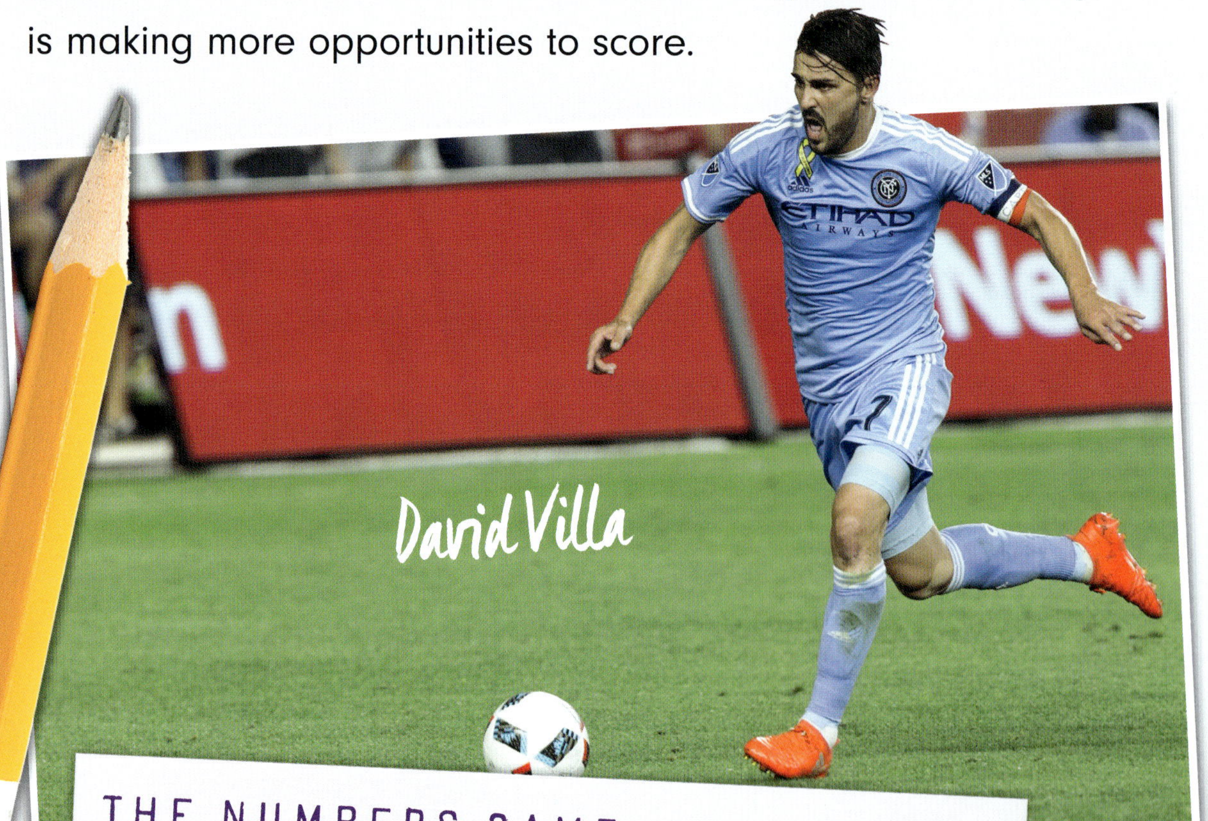

David Villa

## THE NUMBERS GAME

IN 2016, DAVID VILLA PLAYED 33 GAMES WITH THE NEW YORK CITY FOOTBALL CLUB. HE SCORED 23 GOALS AND HAD 68 SHOTS ON GOAL! LET'S SAY A PLAYER MADE 149 SHOTS. IF 87 OF THESE SHOTS WERE NOT ON GOAL, HOW MANY SHOTS ON GOAL DOES THE PLAYER HAVE? ANSWER ON PAGE 29.

Hope Solo blocks a shot on goal.

SOME PEOPLE THINK SHOTS ON GOAL IS AN IMPORTANT STAT, BUT OTHERS DON'T, BECAUSE HAVING MORE SHOTS ON GOAL DOESN'T NECESSARILY MEAN MORE GOALS.

# WORK TOGETHER

Soccer is all about teamwork, so assists are important stats, too. Assists are passes that directly lead to another teammate scoring a goal. For example, let's say Brianna passed the ball to Malcolm and then Malcolm kicked it into the net. Malcolm gets the goal, but Brianna gets the assist because her pass led to Malcolm making the goal.

## BAD STATS

Not all stats are good. If a player breaks a rule, they may be shown a yellow card. Yellow cards **caution** players. If a player is shown 2 yellow cards in a game, or breaks a more serious rule, they get a red card and are kicked out of the game. Yellow and red cards are part of a player's stats, just like goals and assists.

Many people think of soccer as being all about scoring goals, but many of these goals wouldn't happen if it weren't for assists. A stat called game-winning assists (GWA) tracks a player's assists that lead directly to the game-winning goal.

IF A PLAYER GETS A RED CARD, THEY'RE NOT REPLACED. THEIR TEAM MUST CONTINUE THE GAME WITH ONE FEWER PLAYER ON THE FIELD.

*Aaron Barry gets a red card.*

# BLOCKING THE SHOTS

After a ball gets past the defenders, it's up to the goalie to block the shot. The goalie is also the only player in soccer who's allowed to touch the ball with his or her hands.

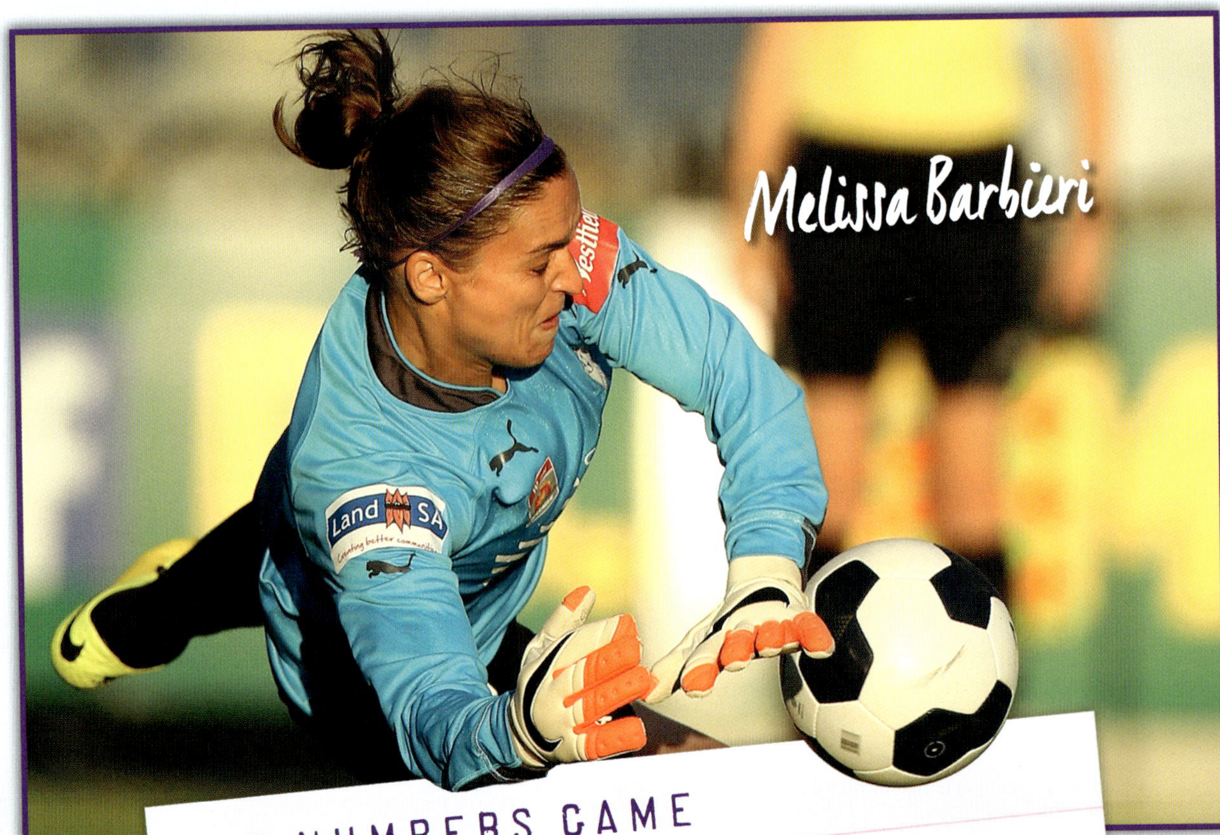

Melissa Barbieri

## THE NUMBERS GAME

LET'S SAY A GOALIE HAS PLAYED 2 GAMES. IN THE FIRST GAME, HE MADE 2 SAVES. IN THE SECOND GAME, HE MADE 4 TIMES THE NUMBER OF SAVES HE MADE IN THE FIRST GAME. HOW MANY TOTAL SAVES HAS HE MADE? ANSWER ON PAGE 29.

THE NUMBER OF SAVES A GOALIE HAS DEPENDS LARGELY ON HOW MANY SHOTS MAKE IT PAST THE OTHER DEFENDERS AND NEAR THE GOAL.

Andre Blake makes a save.

Goalies don't always have to be skilled at the same things the other players do, such as shooting and ball handling. However, they have to have other skills. Goalies need to be fast and have excellent **reflexes**. Goalies are ranked by a stat called saves. A save happens any time a goalie stops or blocks a ball that would have otherwise gone into the goal.

# WHAT'S THE DIFFERENCE?

Stats aren't just for the individual players. Team stats matter, too. A stat called goal **differential** can help show how well a team is doing. To find a team's goal differential, you need to know how many total goals they've made and how many total goals they've conceded, or let into the net. The difference between these two numbers is their goal differential.

A team's goal differential can be positive or negative. A positive goal differential means a team has scored more goals than they've allowed. A negative goal differential means they've been scored on more times than they've scored.

## THE NUMBERS GAME

MANCHESTER UNITED IS A POPULAR TEAM IN THE ENGLISH PREMIER LEAGUE. IN THE 2015–2016 SEASON, THEY HAD 49 GOALS AND CONCEDED 35 GOALS, MAKING THEIR GOAL DIFFERENTIAL +14. IF A TEAM HAD 86 GOALS AND CONCEDED 31, WHAT WOULD THEIR GOAL DIFFERENTIAL BE? ANSWER ON PAGE 29.

THOUGH THE PREMIER LEAGUE ONLY FORMED IN 1992, MANY OF ITS TEAMS, INCLUDING MANCHESTER UNITED, HAVE BEEN AROUND MUCH LONGER.

# CAP IT OFF

Stats like goals and saves have pretty straightforward names. If you know what a goal or a save is, you probably know what the stat means. Some words in soccer don't make as much sense. Maybe you've heard of your favorite player getting their 100th cap, but what does that mean?

Today, teams wear matching shirts when they compete in FIFA matches. Before that was common practice, there were caps. Each time you represented your country in a match you got a cap. The term stuck, and it is still said that a player "earns a cap" every time they play in an international match.

## THE NUMBERS GAME

KRISTINE LILLY IS A FORMER A MEMBER OF THE US WOMEN'S NATIONAL SOCCER TEAM. WITH MORE THAN 350 CAPS TO HER NAME, SHE APPEARED IN MORE INTERNATIONAL SOCCER MATCHES THAN ANY OTHER PLAYER. IF A PLAYER WERE TO PLAY IN 6 INTERNATIONAL MATCHES PER YEAR FOR 13 YEARS, HOW MANY CAPS WOULD THEY HAVE? ANSWER ON PAGE 29.

SOME TEAMS PLAY MORE INTERNATIONAL GAMES THAN OTHERS, MEANING SOME PLAYERS MIGHT HAVE A BETTER SHOT AT GETTING MORE CAPS. FOR MANY, HITTING 100 CAPS IS CONSIDERED A **MILESTONE**.

Former soccer star Nat Lofthouse with his England caps

# A GROWING GAME

Soccer is an action-packed game full of numbers and math! Understanding these stats can help us better follow and enjoy the game.

Soccer's already one of the most loved sports around the world, but in the United States, it's still not quite as popular on the professional level as some other sports, such as football and baseball, but that could change!

### A RISING FAVORITE

In 2014, one study even showed that Major League Soccer was just as popular as Major League Baseball with Americans between 12 and 17 years old. What do you think—does soccer have what it takes to become the next national **pastime** of the United States?

More than 3 million kids play in soccer programs around the United States. That number's risen greatly in the last few **decades**. It might not be long before the game becomes just as popular in the United States as it is in other parts of the world!

## ANSWER KEY

p. 11 – 2,200 square yards
p. 12 – 24 feet
p. 14 – 15 players
p. 17 – 28 goals
p. 18 – 62 shots on goal
p. 22 – 10 total saves
p. 24 – + 55 goal differential
p. 26 – 78 caps

READING ABOUT SOCCER CAN HELP YOU UNDERSTAND THE DIFFERENT STATS, BUT THE BEST WAY TO LEARN ABOUT THE SPORT IS TO PLAY IT!

# GLOSSARY

**calculate:** to figure something out using math

**caution:** to warn

**competition:** an event in which people or teams try to win

**decade:** a period of 10 years

**differential:** a difference between things

**international:** involving two or more countries

**milestone:** an important point in the progress of something

**pastime:** an activity that someone enjoys during their free time

**professional:** earning money from an activity that many people do for fun

**reflexes:** the ability to react quickly

**roster:** the list of people who are on a team

**statistics:** information that can be related in numbers

# FOR MORE INFORMATION

## BOOKS

Mahaney, Ian F. *The Math of Soccer.* New York, NY: PowerKids Press, 2012.

Watson, Stephanie. *The Science Behind Soccer, Volleyball, Cycling, and Other Popular Sports.* North Mankato, MN: Capstone Press, 2016.

## WEBSITES

**Major League Soccer**

*www.mlssoccer.com*

Use this site to keep up with your favorite MLS teams and players—and their latest stats!

**National Women's Soccer League**

*www.nwslsoccer.com*

This website is loaded with facts and stats to keep you updated on all your favorite NWSL teams and players.

**Soccer (Football)**

*www.ducksters.com/sports/soccer.php*

Check out this site for more details about this exciting sport.

**Publisher's note to educators and parents:** Our editors have carefully reviewed these websites to ensure that they are suitable for students. Many websites change frequently, however, and we cannot guarantee that a site's future contents will continue to meet our high standards of quality and educational value. Be advised that students should be closely supervised whenever they access the Internet.

# INDEX